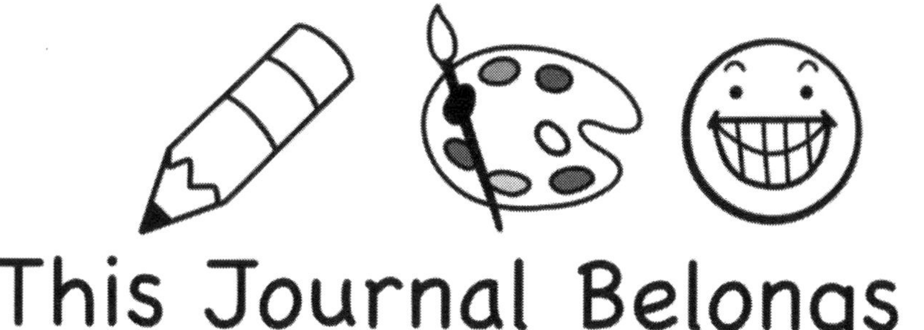

This Journal Belongs To

The Hardest Part Of Today Was:

____

____

____

____

I Handled The Hard Part By:

____

____

____

____

Coping Tools I Used Today

Talk To A Friend

Walk Away & Be By Myself

Draw Or Doodle

Tell An Adult

Write In My Journal

Take Some Deep Breaths

My Good Thoughts

Date:

My Bad Thoughts

My Feelings

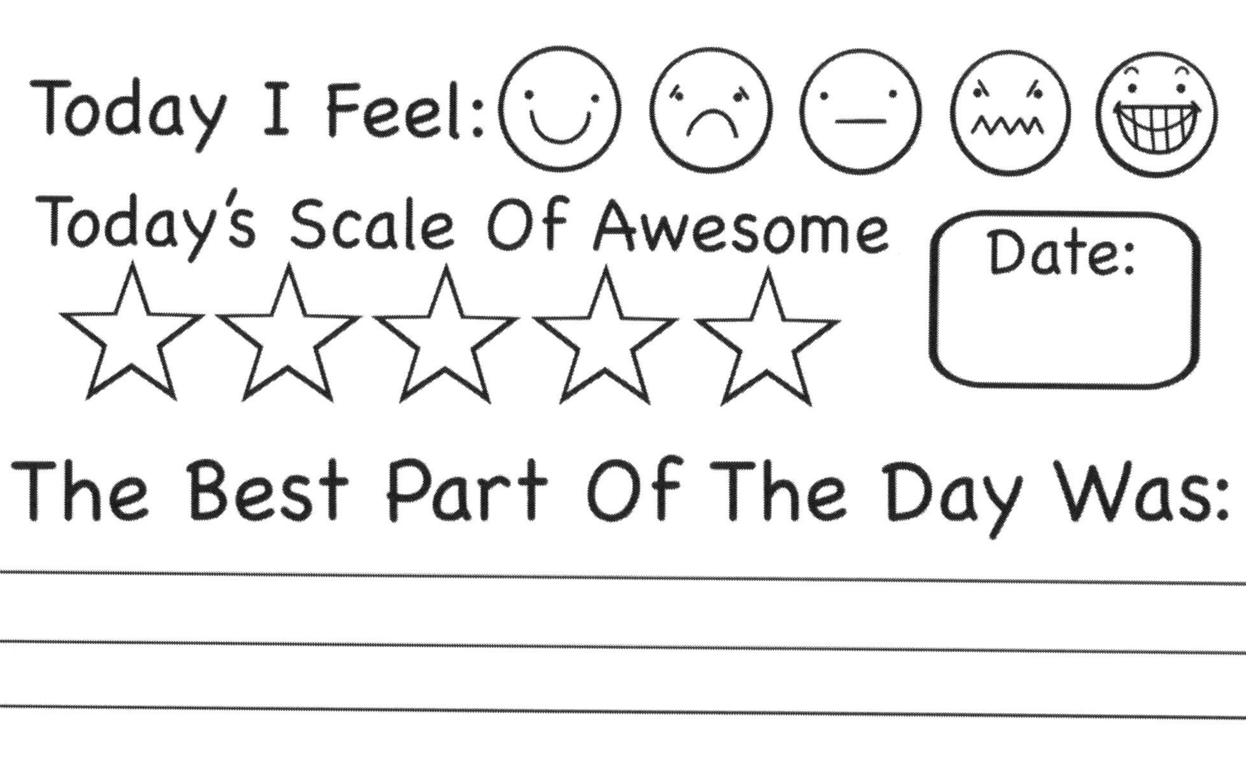
Today I Feel:
Today's Scale Of Awesome
Date:
The Best Part Of The Day Was:

My Doodles 

The Hardest Part Of Today Was:

____

____

____

____

I Handled The Hard Part By:

____

____

____

____

Coping Tools I Used Today

Talk To A Friend

Walk Away & Be By Myself

Draw Or Doodle

Tell An Adult

Write In My Journal

Take Some Deep Breaths

My Good Thoughts

Date:

My Bad Thoughts

My Feelings

Today I Feel:

Today's Scale Of Awesome

Date:

The Best Part Of The Day Was:

My Doodles

The Hardest Part Of Today Was:

____

____

____

____

I Handled The Hard Part By:

____

____

____

____

Coping Tools I Used Today

Talk To A Friend

Walk Away & Be By Myself

Draw Or Doodle

Tell An Adult

Write In My Journal

Take Some Deep Breaths

My Good Thoughts

Date:

My Bad Thoughts

My Feelings

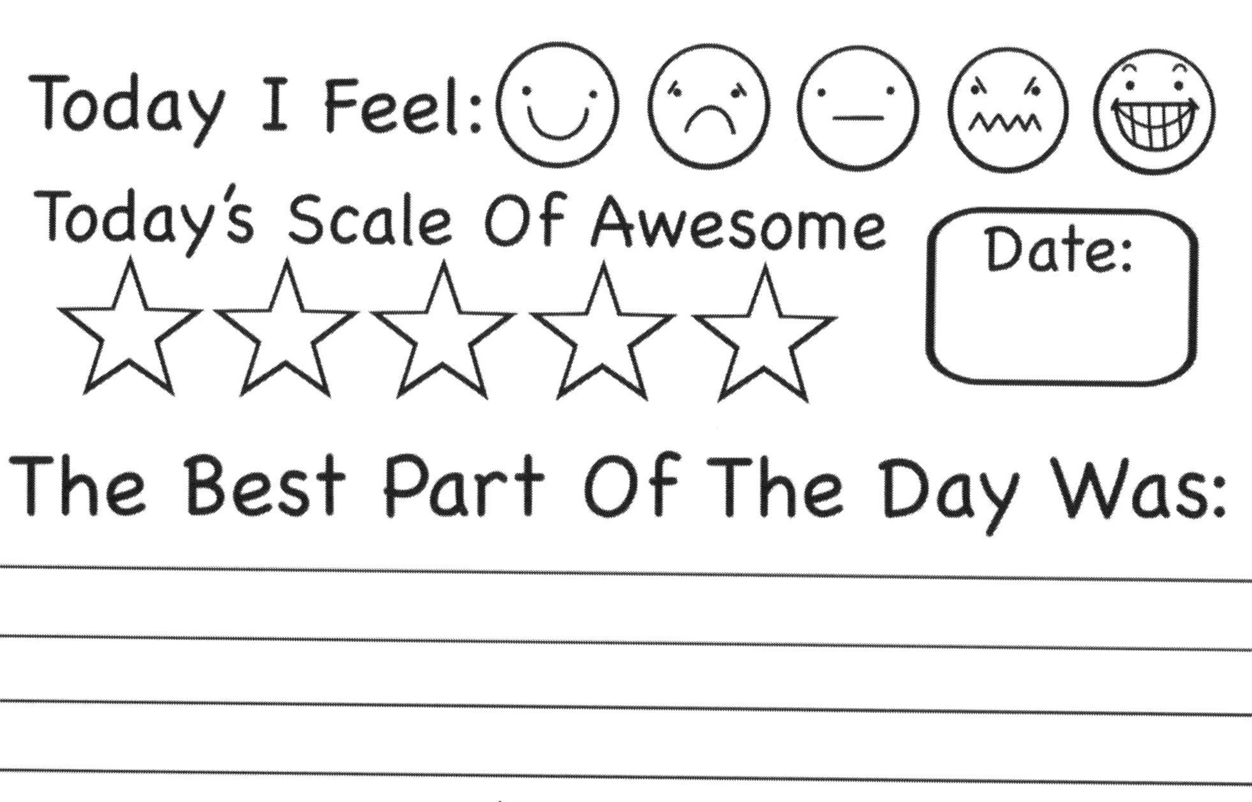
Today I Feel:
Today's Scale Of Awesome
Date:
The Best Part Of The Day Was:

My Doodles 

The Hardest Part Of Today Was:

____

____

____

____

I Handled The Hard Part By:

____

____

____

____

Coping Tools I Used Today

Talk To A Friend

Walk Away & Be By Myself

Draw Or Doodle

Tell An Adult

Write In My Journal

Take Some Deep Breaths

My Good Thoughts

Date:

My Bad Thoughts

My Feelings

Today I Feel:

Today's Scale Of Awesome

Date:

The Best Part Of The Day Was:

My Doodles

The Hardest Part Of Today Was:

____

____

____

____

I Handled The Hard Part By:

____

____

____

____

Coping Tools I Used Today

Talk To A Friend

Walk Away & Be By Myself

Draw Or Doodle

Tell An Adult

Write In My Journal

Take Some Deep Breaths

My Good Thoughts

Date:

My Bad Thoughts

My Feelings

Today I Feel:
Today's Scale Of Awesome
Date:
The Best Part Of The Day Was:

My Doodles 

Today I Feel:

Today's Scale Of Awesome

Date:

The Hardest Part Of Today Was:

____

____

____

____

I Handled The Hard Part By:

____

____

____

____

Coping Tools I Used Today

Talk To A Friend

Walk Away & Be By Myself

Draw Or Doodle

Tell An Adult

Write In My Journal

Take Some Deep Breaths

My Good Thoughts

Date:

My Bad Thoughts

My Feelings

Today I Feel:

Today's Scale Of Awesome

Date:

The Best Part Of The Day Was:

My Doodles

The Hardest Part Of Today Was:

____

____

____

____

I Handled The Hard Part By:

____

____

____

____

Coping Tools I Used Today

Talk To A Friend

Walk Away & Be By Myself

Draw Or Doodle

Tell An Adult

Write In My Journal

Take Some Deep Breaths

My Good Thoughts

Date:

My Bad Thoughts

My Feelings

Today I Feel:
Today's Scale Of Awesome
Date:
The Best Part Of The Day Was:

My Doodles 

The Hardest Part Of Today Was:

____

____

____

____

I Handled The Hard Part By:

____

____

____

____

Coping Tools I Used Today

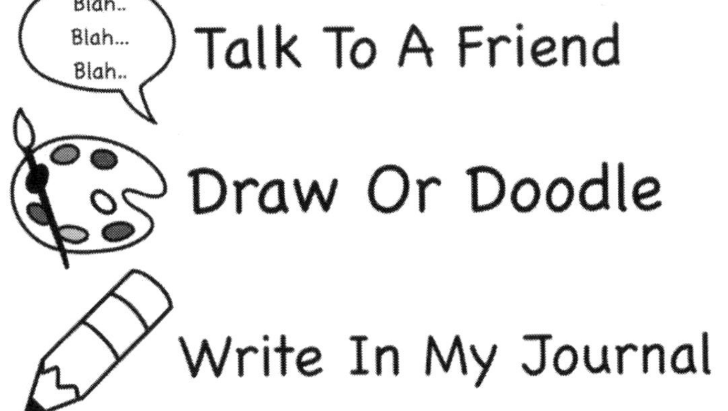

Walk Away & Be By Myself

Tell An Adult

Take Some Deep Breaths

My Good Thoughts

Date:

My Bad Thoughts

My Feelings

Today I Feel:

Today's Scale Of Awesome

Date:

The Best Part Of The Day Was:

My Doodles

The Hardest Part Of Today Was:

____

____

____

____

I Handled The Hard Part By:

____

____

____

____

Coping Tools I Used Today

Talk To A Friend

Walk Away & Be By Myself

Draw Or Doodle

Tell An Adult

Write In My Journal

Take Some Deep Breaths

My Good Thoughts

Date:

My Bad Thoughts

My Feelings

Today I Feel:
Today's Scale Of Awesome
Date:
The Best Part Of The Day Was:

My Doodles

The Hardest Part Of Today Was:

____

____

____

____

I Handled The Hard Part By:

____

____

____

____

Coping Tools I Used Today

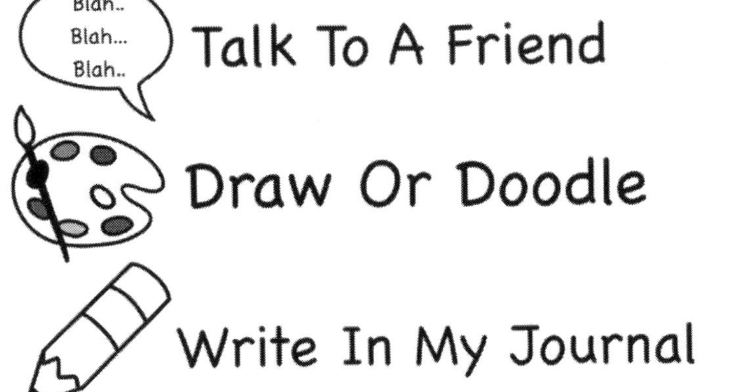

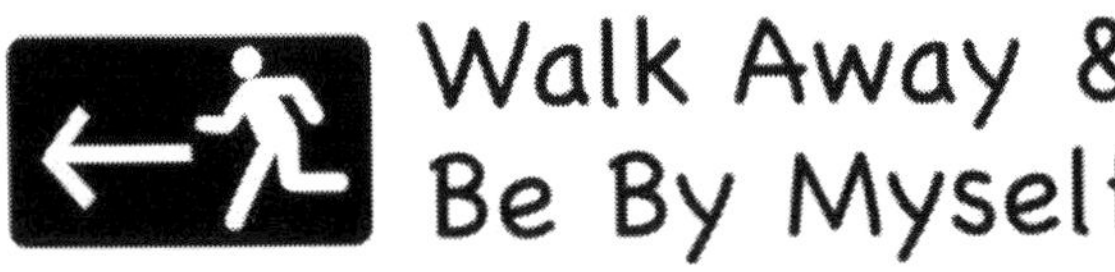

My Good Thoughts

Date:

My Bad Thoughts

My Feelings

Today I Feel:

Today's Scale Of Awesome

Date:

The Best Part Of The Day Was:

My Doodles

The Hardest Part Of Today Was:

I Handled The Hard Part By:

Coping Tools I Used Today

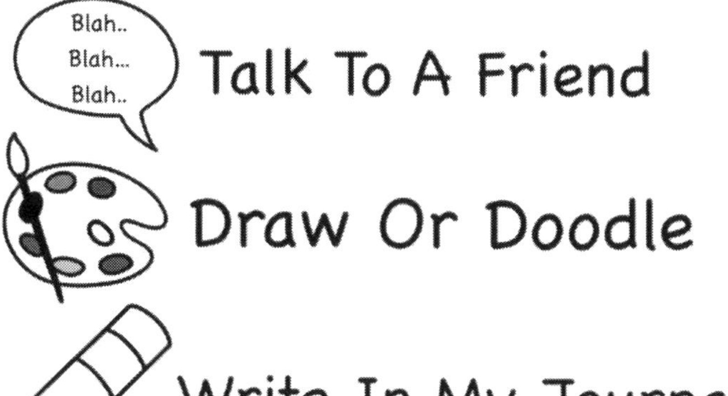

Talk To A Friend

Walk Away & Be By Myself

Draw Or Doodle

Tell An Adult

Write In My Journal

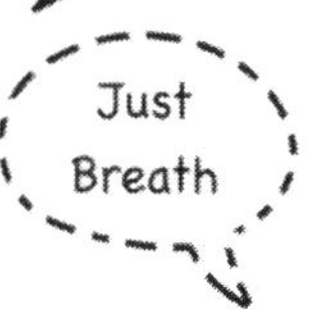

Take Some Deep Breaths

My Good Thoughts

Date:

My Bad Thoughts

My Feelings

Today I Feel:

Today's Scale Of Awesome

Date:

The Best Part Of The Day Was:

My Doodles

The Hardest Part Of Today Was:

____

____

____

____

I Handled The Hard Part By:

____

____

____

____

Coping Tools I Used Today

Talk To A Friend

Walk Away & Be By Myself

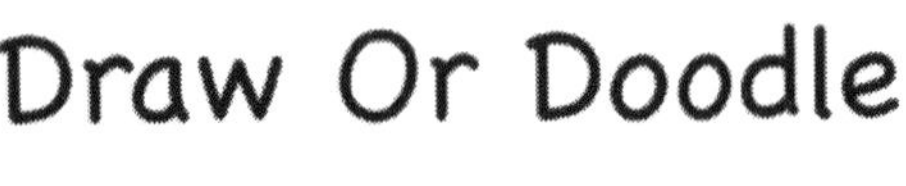

Draw Or Doodle

Tell An Adult

Write In My Journal

Take Some Deep Breaths

My Good Thoughts

Date:

My Bad Thoughts

My Feelings

Today I Feel:

Today's Scale Of Awesome

Date:

The Best Part Of The Day Was:

My Doodles

The Hardest Part Of Today Was:

____

____

____

____

I Handled The Hard Part By:

____

____

____

____

Coping Tools I Used Today

Talk To A Friend

Draw Or Doodle

Write In My Journal

Walk Away & Be By Myself

Tell An Adult

Take Some Deep Breaths

My Good Thoughts

Date:

My Bad Thoughts

My Feelings

The Best Part Of The Day Was:

My Doodles

The Hardest Part Of Today Was:

____

____

____

____

I Handled The Hard Part By:

____

____

____

____

Coping Tools I Used Today

Talk To A Friend

Walk Away & Be By Myself

Draw Or Doodle

Tell An Adult

Write In My Journal

Take Some Deep Breaths

My Good Thoughts

Date:

My Bad Thoughts

My Feelings

Today I Feel:

Today's Scale Of Awesome

Date:

The Best Part Of The Day Was:

My Doodles

The Hardest Part Of Today Was:

____

____

____

____

I Handled The Hard Part By:

____

____

____

____

Coping Tools I Used Today

Talk To A Friend

Walk Away & Be By Myself

Draw Or Doodle

Tell An Adult

Write In My Journal

Take Some Deep Breaths

My Good Thoughts

Date:

My Bad Thoughts

My Feelings

Today I Feel:

Today's Scale Of Awesome

Date:

The Best Part Of The Day Was:

My Doodles

The Hardest Part Of Today Was:

____

____

____

____

I Handled The Hard Part By:

____

____

____

____

Coping Tools I Used Today

Talk To A Friend

Walk Away & Be By Myself

Draw Or Doodle

Tell An Adult

Write In My Journal

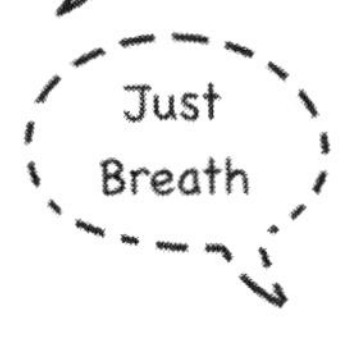

Take Some Deep Breaths

My Good Thoughts

Date:

My Bad Thoughts

My Feelings

Today I Feel:

Today's Scale Of Awesome

Date:

The Best Part Of The Day Was:

My Doodles

The Hardest Part Of Today Was:

I Handled The Hard Part By:

Coping Tools I Used Today

Talk To A Friend

Walk Away & Be By Myself

Draw Or Doodle

Tell An Adult

Write In My Journal

Take Some Deep Breaths

My Good Thoughts

Date:

My Bad Thoughts

My Feelings

Today I Feel:

Today's Scale Of Awesome

Date:

The Best Part Of The Day Was:

My Doodles

The Hardest Part Of Today Was:

____

____

____

____

I Handled The Hard Part By:

____

____

____

____

Coping Tools I Used Today

Talk To A Friend

Walk Away & Be By Myself

Draw Or Doodle

Tell An Adult

Write In My Journal

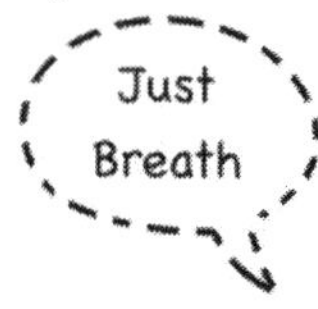

Take Some Deep Breaths

My Good Thoughts

Date:

My Bad Thoughts

My Feelings

Today I Feel:
Today's Scale Of Awesome
Date:
The Best Part Of The Day Was:

My Doodles 

The Hardest Part Of Today Was:

____

____

____

____

I Handled The Hard Part By:

____

____

____

____

Coping Tools I Used Today

Talk To A Friend

Walk Away & Be By Myself

Draw Or Doodle

Tell An Adult

Write In My Journal

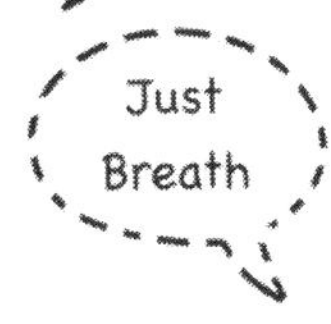

Take Some Deep Breaths

My Good Thoughts

Date:

My Bad Thoughts

My Feelings

Today I Feel:

Today's Scale Of Awesome

Date:

The Best Part Of The Day Was:

My Doodles

The Hardest Part Of Today Was:

____

____

____

____

I Handled The Hard Part By:

____

____

____

____

Coping Tools I Used Today

Talk To A Friend

Walk Away & Be By Myself

Draw Or Doodle

Tell An Adult

Write In My Journal

Take Some Deep Breaths

My Good Thoughts

Date:

My Bad Thoughts

My Feelings

Today I Feel:
Today's Scale Of Awesome
Date:
The Best Part Of The Day Was:

My Doodles 

The Hardest Part Of Today Was:

____

____

____

____

I Handled The Hard Part By:

____

____

____

____

Coping Tools I Used Today

Talk To A Friend

Walk Away & Be By Myself

Draw Or Doodle

Tell An Adult

Write In My Journal

Take Some Deep Breaths

My Good Thoughts

Date:

My Bad Thoughts

My Feelings

Today I Feel:

Today's Scale Of Awesome

Date:

The Best Part Of The Day Was:

My Doodles 

The Hardest Part Of Today Was:

I Handled The Hard Part By:

Coping Tools I Used Today

Talk To A Friend

Walk Away & Be By Myself

Draw Or Doodle

Tell An Adult

Write In My Journal

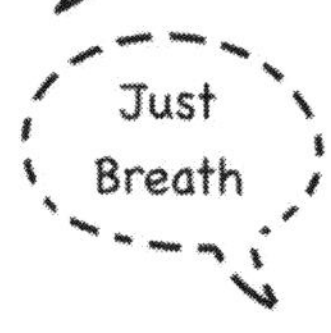

Take Some Deep Breaths

My Good Thoughts

Date:

My Bad Thoughts

My Feelings

Today I Feel:

Today's Scale Of Awesome

Date:

The Best Part Of The Day Was:

My Doodles 

The Hardest Part Of Today Was:

____

____

____

____

I Handled The Hard Part By:

____

____

____

____

Coping Tools I Used Today

Talk To A Friend

Walk Away & Be By Myself

Draw Or Doodle

Tell An Adult

Write In My Journal

Take Some Deep Breaths

My Good Thoughts

Date:

My Bad Thoughts

My Feelings

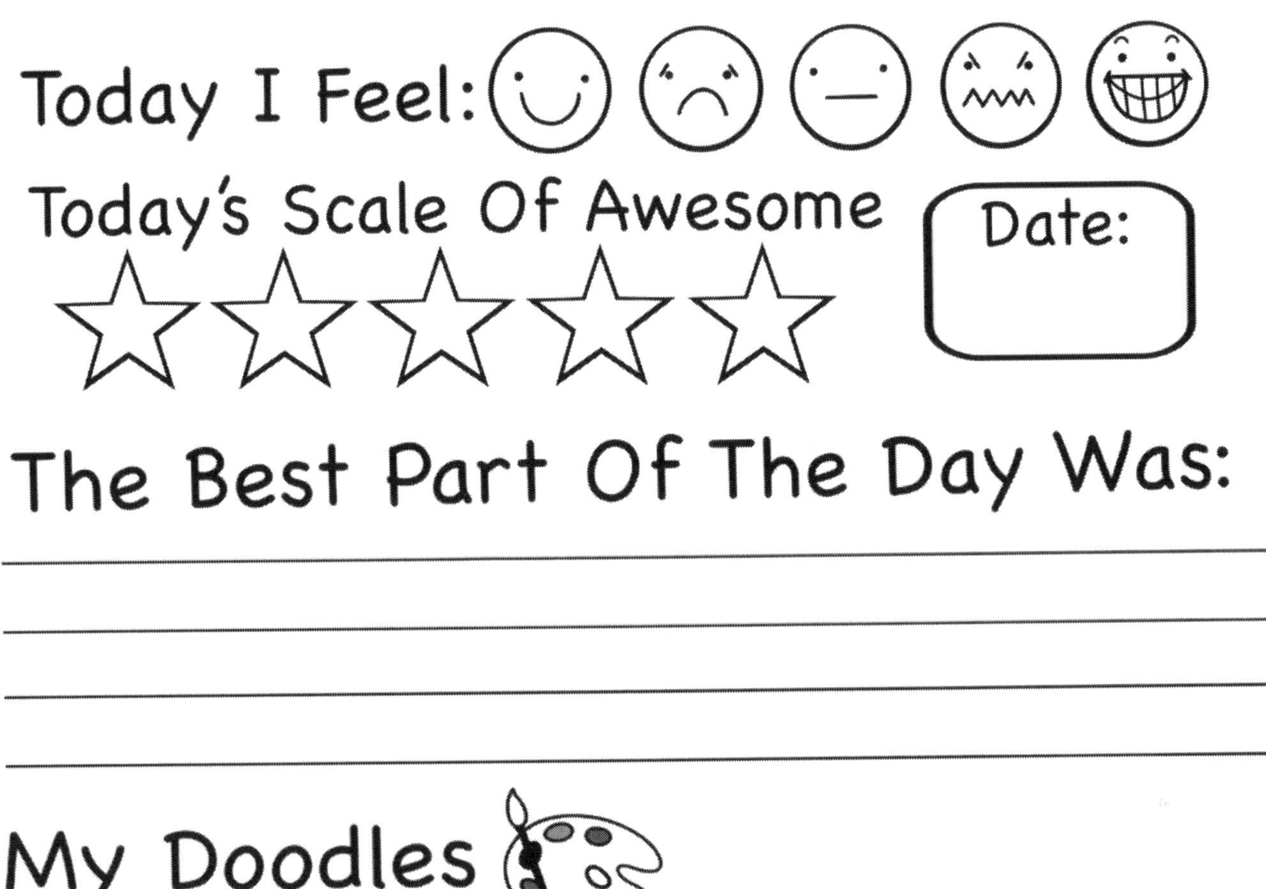

Today I Feel:

Today's Scale Of Awesome

Date:

The Best Part Of The Day Was:

My Doodles

The Hardest Part Of Today Was:

I Handled The Hard Part By:

Coping Tools I Used Today

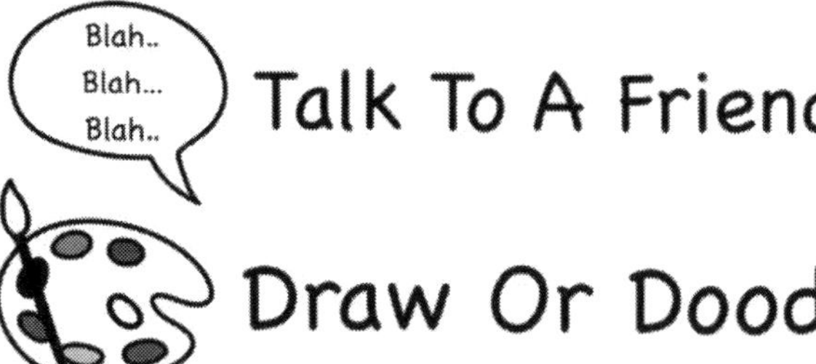

Talk To A Friend

Walk Away & Be By Myself

Draw Or Doodle

Tell An Adult

Write In My Journal

Take Some Deep Breaths

My Good Thoughts

Date:

My Bad Thoughts

My Feelings

Today I Feel:

Today's Scale Of Awesome

Date:

The Best Part Of The Day Was:

My Doodles 

The Hardest Part Of Today Was:

____

____

____

____

I Handled The Hard Part By:

____

____

____

____

Coping Tools I Used Today

Talk To A Friend

Walk Away & Be By Myself

Draw Or Doodle

Tell An Adult

Write In My Journal

Take Some Deep Breaths

My Good Thoughts

Date:

My Bad Thoughts

My Feelings

Today I Feel:

Today's Scale Of Awesome

Date:

The Best Part Of The Day Was:

My Doodles

The Hardest Part Of Today Was:

____

____

____

____

I Handled The Hard Part By:

____

____

____

____

Coping Tools I Used Today

Talk To A Friend

Walk Away & Be By Myself

Draw Or Doodle

Tell An Adult

Write In My Journal

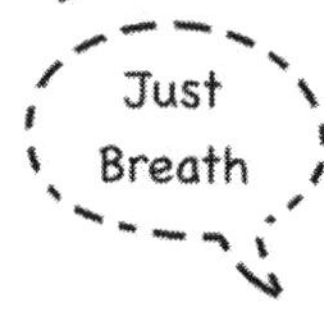

Take Some Deep Breaths

My Good Thoughts

Date:

My Bad Thoughts

My Feelings

Today I Feel:
Today's Scale Of Awesome
Date:
The Best Part Of The Day Was:

My Doodles 

The Hardest Part Of Today Was:

I Handled The Hard Part By:

Coping Tools I Used Today

Talk To A Friend

Walk Away & Be By Myself

Draw Or Doodle

Tell An Adult

Write In My Journal

Take Some Deep Breaths

My Good Thoughts

Date:

My Bad Thoughts

My Feelings

Today I Feel:

Today's Scale Of Awesome

Date:

The Best Part Of The Day Was:

My Doodles

The Hardest Part Of Today Was:

I Handled The Hard Part By:

Coping Tools I Used Today

Talk To A Friend

Walk Away & Be By Myself

Draw Or Doodle

Tell An Adult

Write In My Journal

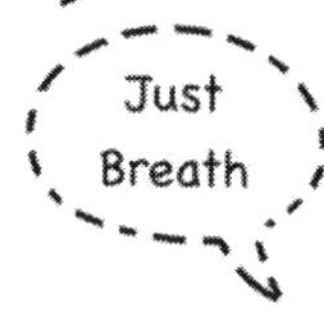

Take Some Deep Breaths

My Good Thoughts

Date:

My Bad Thoughts

My Feelings

Today I Feel:

Today's Scale Of Awesome

Date:

The Best Part Of The Day Was:

My Doodles

The Hardest Part Of Today Was:

____

____

____

____

I Handled The Hard Part By:

____

____

____

____

Coping Tools I Used Today

Talk To A Friend

Walk Away & Be By Myself

Draw Or Doodle

Tell An Adult

Write In My Journal

Take Some Deep Breaths

My Good Thoughts

Date:

My Bad Thoughts

My Feelings

Today I Feel:

Today's Scale Of Awesome

Date:

The Best Part Of The Day Was:

My Doodles

The Hardest Part Of Today Was:

____

____

____

____

I Handled The Hard Part By:

____

____

____

____

Coping Tools I Used Today

Talk To A Friend

Walk Away & Be By Myself

Draw Or Doodle

Tell An Adult

Write In My Journal

Take Some Deep Breaths

My Good Thoughts

Date:

My Bad Thoughts

My Feelings

Today I Feel:

Today's Scale Of Awesome

Date:

The Best Part Of The Day Was:

My Doodles 

The Hardest Part Of Today Was:

I Handled The Hard Part By:

Coping Tools I Used Today

Talk To A Friend

Walk Away & Be By Myself

Draw Or Doodle

Tell An Adult

Write In My Journal

Take Some Deep Breaths

My Good Thoughts

Date:

My Bad Thoughts

My Feelings

Today I Feel:

Today's Scale Of Awesome

Date:

The Best Part Of The Day Was:

My Doodles

The Hardest Part Of Today Was:

____

____

____

____

I Handled The Hard Part By:

____

____

____

____

Coping Tools I Used Today

Talk To A Friend

Walk Away & Be By Myself

Draw Or Doodle

Tell An Adult

Write In My Journal

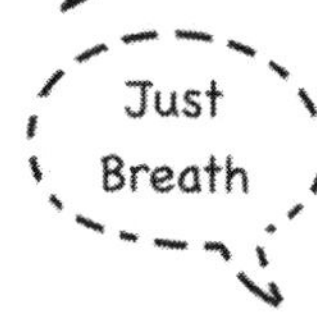

Take Some Deep Breaths

My Good Thoughts

Date:

My Bad Thoughts

My Feelings

Today I Feel:
Today's Scale Of Awesome
Date:
The Best Part Of The Day Was:

My Doodles 

The Hardest Part Of Today Was:

____

____

____

____

I Handled The Hard Part By:

____

____

____

____

Coping Tools I Used Today

Talk To A Friend

Walk Away & Be By Myself

Draw Or Doodle

Tell An Adult

Write In My Journal

Take Some Deep Breaths

My Good Thoughts

Date:

My Bad Thoughts

My Feelings

Today I Feel:
Today's Scale Of Awesome
Date:
The Best Part Of The Day Was:

My Doodles

Made in the USA
Lexington, KY
19 September 2018